how to
PREPARE
PERFORM &
PASS
an
ISO 9001:2015
audit
2020 edition

Copyright © 2020 Rhys J Mitchell

All rights reserved. No part of this book may be reproduced or transmitted in any form or by any means, electronic or mechanical, including photocopying, recording, or by an information storage and retrieval system - except by a reviewer who may quote brief passages in a review to be printed in a magazine or newspaper - without permission in writing from the publisher.

ISBN: 9798618615969

DEDICATION

To the one, Laurice, who is always there, and the ones who have always been there; Mary, Simon and Conor.

contents
INTRODUCTION 1
COMMON QUESTIONS 3
THE ISO 9001:2015 STANDARD 17
PLAN-DO-CHECK-ACT 19
SECTION-BY-SECTION 25
PREPARING FOR THE AUDIT 49
THE MANDATORY PARTS 51
PREPARING YOUR TEAM 57
TIPS FOR THE DAY & AUDIT SKILLS 67
CLOSING THOUGHTS 81
APPENDICES 85
ORGANISATIONAL RISK REGISTER 87
INTERESTED PARTIES 95
ABOUT THE AUTHOR 99

INTRODUCTION

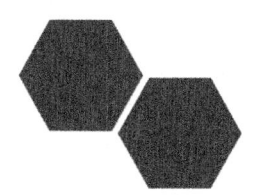

COMMON QUESTIONS

So, you are being audited.

It is OK, it is perfectly normal, it happens to every organisation sometimes.

For the past ten years, I have been either preparing for an audit, being audited, or just finished one and are planning for the next audit. Fortunately, most of them have gone very well.

When training people to be ready for audits I

always tell them one thing; you don't need to panic, but you do need to prepare.

That is where this book comes in.

Why this book?

This book will help you prepare for an ISO 9001:2015 Quality Management System audit. You may have heard of ISO 9001, you may even know what it means; but if you haven't, that is OK.

This book won't break down the ISO 9001:2015 Quality Management System Standard clause-by-clause, but it will prepare you, and more importantly, help you understand what you need to prepare.

What is ISO?

ISO is the International Organisation of Standardisation; they are an independent, global organisation dedicated to the development and publication of International Standards.

So, what does ISO stand for?

Nothing, it's an abbreviation, not an acronym. It derives from the Greek word isos; meaning equal, or consistent.

So what is an International Standard?

They are technical guidelines developed by ISO (and other international organisations such as the World Health Organisation), made public and free; intended to provide guidance and systems of best-practice in industry and commerce.

How can they help?

In the mid- to late- 19th century, many new companies entered the electrical markets. Each chose their own settings for voltage, frequency and current. Even technical drawings used bespoke symbols. As a result, electrical systems in adjacent buildings would be completely incompatible because they were fitted by different companies.

This led to the creation of the first international standards organization, the International

Electrotechnical Commission, which standardised technical specifications and electrical measurements. The IEC guided companies, removing inefficiencies, reducing costs and increasing safety.

In time, the International Organisation of Standardisation formed after World War II, dedicated to enhancing international cooperation for technical standards and specifications.

You see the effects of International Standards today whenever you go on holiday, for example:

Commercial aeroplanes are made by different manufacturers and run by different airlines, but they all basically look the same, and the experience of flying is broadly the same between them. The reason being, they all have to follow the same standard to be approved to fly. This removes the burden of developing the best practice from the individual companies, reducing costs and increasing efficiency and safety.

What is ISO 9001:2015?

If you have heard of one of the 20,000+ International Standards developed by ISO, it will probably be ISO 9001. It is extremely popular and used worldwide.

It is the key standard of the family of the Quality Management System (QMS) standards. From ISO.org, an ISO 9001 organisation:

a) needs to demonstrate its ability to consistently provide products and services that meet customer and applicable statutory and regulatory requirements, and

b) aims to enhance customer satisfaction through the effective application of the system, including processes for improvement of the system and the assurance of conformity to customer and applicable statutory and regulatory requirements.

In essence, ISO 9001 is about the organisation providing an equal (consistent) and satisfying experience for the customer.

ISO 9001 refers to the Standard. 2015 refers to its last revision.

Why is it so popular?

Although it has its origins, in manufacturing, it was expanded to be generic and applicable to any organisation, regardless of size and type of product or service it provides.

Don't be put off by the world quality though, ISO 9001 is closer to a business management standard, and provides guidance and best-practice for all departments in your organisation.

If you take a look at the key principles below, you can see how focusing on these can benefit all organisations.

Key Principles of ISO 9001:2015

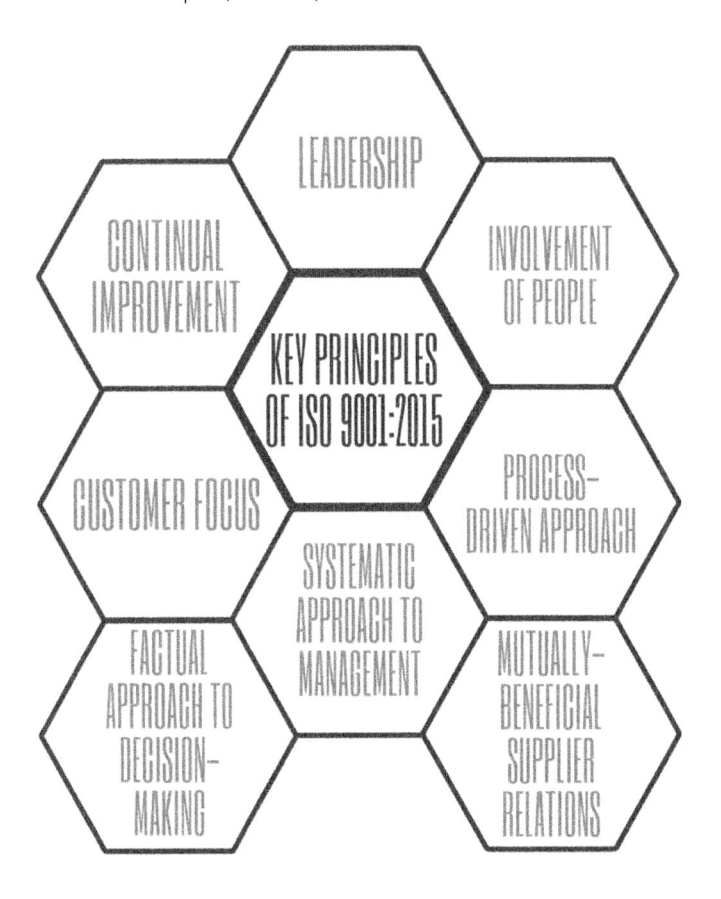

- Leadership
- Continual Improvement
- Involvement of People
- Customer Focus
- Process-Driven Approach
- Factual Approach to Decision-Making
- Systematic Approach to Management
- Mutually-Beneficial Supplier Relations

What is an audit?

Any organisation can (and probably should) follow ISO 9001's key principles, however, in order to be certified, you will need to be audited to the Standard.

Audit frequency and duration will vary depending on the size and complexity, but broadly speaking the process will be the same.

The typical audit process

A third-party company (for example, BSI or SGS) will visit your business to assess compliance to the ISO 9001 Standard. Some parts of the Standard are mandatory, some will depend on your own processes, but the key things they are looking for are compliance and consistency.

Essentially, they want you to plan what you do, and do what you plan.

There are three types of audit: certification, re-certification, and surveillance.

If your organisation doesn't already have ISO 9001 accreditation, you will need to have a *certification audit*. The auditor will confirm compliance with the mandatory sections of the Standard, and review all of your processes; in other words, department-by-department. Typically, this will be your longest audit and require the most preparation.

Following certification, you will continue to have *surveillance audits* are regular intervals (which depends on the size and complexity of your organisation). These are smaller in scope, focusing on only a few processes in addition to the mandatory requirements.

Throughout the cycle of the certificate; all processes will be covered though. For instance, in one surveillance audit, Warehousing and Customer Service may be covered, whereas next time, Purchasing and Repairs would be. Certain processes, such as management meetings and faulty goods complaints, will always be audited. More on this in the **Preparing for the Audit** chapter.

ISO 9001 certificates are valid for three years. Before they are due to expire, you will need a *recertification audit.* This is not too dissimilar from the surveillance audits: in addition to processes reviewed on the day, the auditor will also review the adults from the three-year cycle, and will make their recommendations for recertification based on this.

What do I get out of it?

If the audit goes well, you will get a certificate of compliance to the ISO 9001:2015 Standard.

What does my certificate mean?

Your certificate shows you comply with the Standard, and it gives confidence to customers and suppliers that you are focused on the eight key principles mentioned before.

How does this benefit you?

Your certificate tells customers and suppliers that you do what you say you do; therefore they do not need to worry about doing their own audit and quality checks. For this reason, a lot of business tenders will require ISO 9001 certification.

What can go wrong?

Worst case scenario is that the auditor finds multiple examples of noncompliance to the audit, and therefore recommends that you are not certified.

A nonconformity is a failure to meet requirements; this could be a customer's requirement, regulatory, from the Standard, or your own: remember, do what you plan, and plan what you do. If you plan to do a management meeting once a month and you don't, that could be a nonconformity.

There are two types of nonconformity; major and minor.

A *minor nonconformity* is an incident in which requirements were not met, but that did not have a large, negative consequence; and therefore doesn't majorly weaken your Quality Management System.

A *major nonconformity* is when there is an absence or a complete breakdown in your Quality Management System, resulting in a wider failure to meet requirements.

For instance, if you were required to inspect a piece of machinery daily and keep a record of such; failure to do so on one or two days out of the year would be a minor nonconformity. Failure to do so for days at a time, multiple times would be a major nonconformity.

What happens with a nonconformity?

Much like your driving test, you are allowed a small number of minors, and maybe a major; depending on the size of the company. If you are a global company with a week-long audit, you will likely be allowed a small number of major nonconformities. Too many though, and the auditor may recommend that you not be accredited.

That is the last resort though. A few minor nonconformities should not affect your certification, however, you must react and control and correct it. This includes determining the root causes; taking corrective and preventative steps to stop it from recurring, and evaluating the effectiveness of your actions, i.e. has it worked.

For ISO 9001 audits, minor nonconformities will always be brought up at the next audit to ensure the steps listed above have been taken. In the case of majors, you may be required to bring the auditor back in to evaluate the steps taken are effective.

So, what do I need to do?

You don't need to panic, but you do need to prepare.

Reading this book is a good start.

In the next few chapters, we will discuss the ISO 9001 Standard and help you understand it in plain English, and also how it fits into your business. We'll then discuss what preparations you need to make before the audit, and then what to expect on the day.

Finally, we will discuss tips and best practice for audits, that you can also pass onto your colleagues.

THE ISO 9001:2015 STANDARD

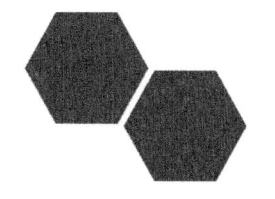

PLAN-DO-CHECK-ACT

Standards are written by technical experts and academics and are hard to wrap your head around. They read like an iTunes user-agreement.

In this chapter, we will break down the Standard into the Plan-Do-Check-Act cycle and Section-by-Section.

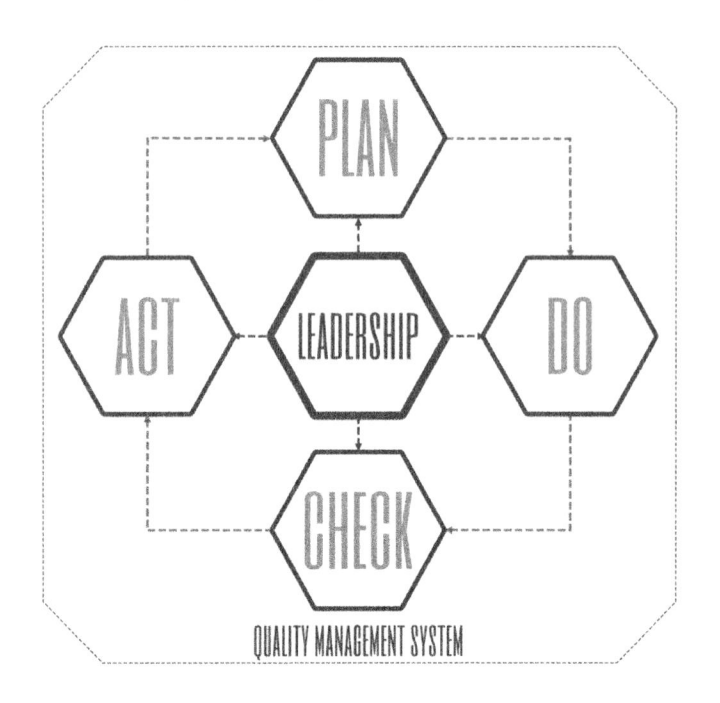

Plan-Do-Check-Act (PDCA) is a management method used in business; emphasising control of processes and products and their continuous improvement.

Control of processes and continuous improvement are two key aspects ISO 9001:2015. Planning your processes around the PDCA cycle will help you a lot with audits, remember; plan what you do, and do what you plan.

If your organisation is a good one, you are probably doing this anyway, you might not even realise it. This book isn't about the PDCA, what follows briefly summarises the cycle so you can understand how it fits with ISO 9001:

Plan

Establish objectives and processes required to deliver the desired results; what you want to do and how you are going to do it. This will be your organisations' financial goals, five-year plans, one-year plans, and other goals, such as those related to sustainability or social causes.

These are typically decided by top management, and relate to section five in the standard; Leadership, and section six; Planning.

Remember, *plan what you do...*

Do

...and do what you plan.

Plan what you do; do what you plan

This is when you enact your plans. It includes, but is not exclusive to, production of goods or provision of services.

If your company manufactures circuit boards, your DO obviously includes their physical manufacture; however, all other departments are doing based on their own plans too.

Procurement buy the parts; that's their DO, but how much they buy and who from is determined by the planning phase; are they going to hold a lot of stock, or very few? Are they buying from a broad pool of suppliers, or a select few?

These are your organisations plans to make; the auditor will be concerned with how you are enacting these plans and if you have appropriate resources to do so. This relates to sections seven and eight of the Standard; Support and Operation.

Check

In this phase, your organisation confirms if you are following the plans made and if they are successful.

For instance, you have planned to have a turnaround time for customer orders of no more than two days. To do this, Customer Service process orders in less than one hour and the Warehouse team will ship the products on next-day delivery.

Your organisation needs to check that you are meeting these targets and if these processes are effective within your long-term plans.

The better you can articulate the effectiveness of your plans, the smoother the audit will go, so have your data ready!

Check relates to Section Nine of the Standard; Performance Evaluation.

Act (or Adjust)

This is where your processes are continually improved. This may include addressing problems, failure to meet targets, nonconformities, inefficiencies, or addressing unforeseen challenges; all with the goal of making the process better and more standardised.

From there, the cycle begins again, and you plan changes from what you learned during the check phase, and implement them into your plans.

This relates to the Improvement chapter if the Standard; Section Ten.

This should give you a bit more understanding of the PDCA cycle; something your organisation likely already does. Having it clear in your mind though will help you better articulate it to the auditor, giving them confidence in your organisation.

SECTION-BY-SECTION

This chapter explains and summarises each section of the ISO 9001:2015 Standard. Consider using this as an accompaniment to the Standard, and as you read divide each clause into departments. Some apply to the entire organisation, though some apply to specific processes and departments.

Doing so will help you plan your internal audits and also prepare the departments on what to expect during the audit.

Beginning

Section One outlines the broad scope of the Standard. Sections Two and Three explain the terminology and definitions. The next section is where it really begins.

Section Four - Context

Section Four does not strictly fit into the PDCA cycle, but remains a critical chapter. It informs all other steps and requires an understanding of the organisation's business environment.

Firstly, you will need to set the scope of your audit; the wording of which will be on your certificate. If your company makes and sells sponges, the scope of your audit may be:

"The design, manufacture and sale of cleaning equipment"

Not all of your processes need to be included in your scope: they won't be audited and therefore won't be certified.

You will need to determine your scope, and exclude any clauses from the Standard that don't apply to you.

Understanding Your Organisation's Context

Consider the internal and external risks and opportunities that affect the organisation.

This is one model you can use to consider and categorise your organisation's risks, and document them in an Organisation Risk Register:

Within each category you can identify specific risks, document the potential impact and likelihood of occurrence, and any existing, mitigating factors. From this, assess if any further actions are needed. Once completed, assess the risks again.

See Appendix One for a more detailed look at how to create an Organisational Risk Register.

Clarify Expectations of Interested Parties

Interested Parties

Interested Parties are a person or organisation that can affect, be affected by, or perceive itself to be affected by a decision or activity (ISO 14001)

The concept of Interested Parties extends beyond a focus solely on the customer. It is important to consider all relevant interested parties... The relevant interested parties are those that provide significant risk to organizational sustainability if their needs and expectations are not met (ISO 9000)

The Six Markets Model can help you identify and

categorise Interested Parties:

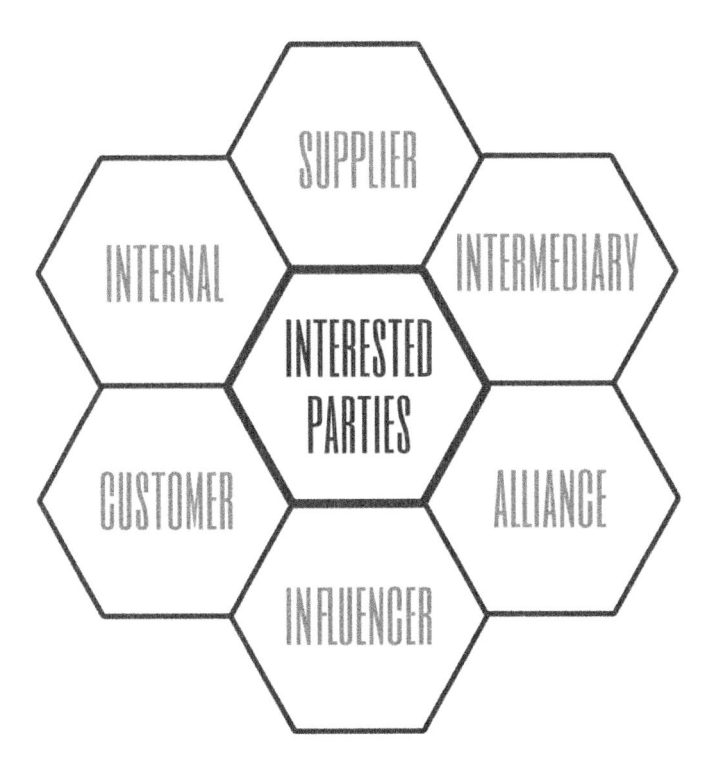

Supplier, Internal, Intermediary, Customer, Alliance, Influencer — Interested Parties

Then, identify their Needs and Expectations, assess to what extent you are meeting them, and any further actions you should take.

The Appendix can give you further information on Interested Parties.

Develop a Quality Management System (QMS)

From your Scope, your organisation will also have its Risks and Opportunities, leading to its Objectives. How are you going to meet these; Standard Operating Procedures (SOPs), management meetings, regular training?

You can decide, but remember, *plan what you do and do what you plan.* If you feel an annual meeting with Top Management is sufficient to discuss the Quality Management System, that is acceptable, just make sure you do it.

There are a few documents that we have already mentioned that you will need for your Quality Manual; you must show you have considered Interested Parties, your Scope, Exclusions, and Risks and Opportunities.

> **Get a date in the diary**
>
> If an auditor asks when you plan to do something, it is better to have a date booked, rather than say "next month"... even if you end up changing it.
>
> Anticipate before the audit and put something in the calendar.

Section Five - Leadership

Leadership (Top Management) will need to demonstrate a focus on Quality and Customers.

To do so, the organisation could have targets relating to customer satisfaction, product quality, and customer complaint response. Leadership should proactively push a customer focus to all staff.

Quality Policy

Your Quality Policy should include the mission or goal of your organisation, demonstrate a commitment to customers and quality, collect the inputs of interested parties, include the required information of 9001, and be communicated to staff.

It is a good idea to pin physical copies in communal areas (kitchens) and remind staff where they are before the audit.

Defining QMS Roles and Responsibilities

Top Leadership can establish a commitment to

the Quality Management System (QMS) by empowering staff members to be responsible for it and providing appropriate support. Someone in the organisation is responsible for the Quality Management System, and if you are reading this book, I have good news for you... it is you. Congratulations!

Leadership is supporting the Quality Management System by putting you in charge of it, and (hopefully) giving you appropriate resources; this means the time you use to support your system, perform audits, as well as training others.

Likely, you will have an internal audit team; you can't audit your own work, so you will need someone else to help you.

Section Six - Planning

This is the *plan* part of the PDCA cycle.

What are your organisation's goals and how are you going to meet them, taking into consideration these risks and opportunities. This could mean the quarter, year or even five-year plan.

This applies to each department also; how do they plan their work? Are these in line with the wider organisation's goals?

The auditor will ask what goals or targets the department has, how they plan to meet them, and how far along they are.

An example of goals

Procurement has a target to reduce their supplier based from 20 to 10 by the end of the year. The auditor will question the Procurement Manager how they are doing this, and how successful they have been. If you are approaching the deadline and still have 15+ suppliers, the auditor will likely challenge if your planning and actions have been appropriate.

Keep in mind, the auditors can only challenge you on your goals; so plan what you do, and do what you plan.

> **Auditors can only challenge; not change**

This is not to say you cannot change your mind. The auditor may revisit you next year, and see from their notes that last year, Procurement had a goal to cut costs by 10%, which you have not done. However, this was not due to poor planning and execution, but the introduction of new, more expensive technology, meant that this was no longer feasible, desirable, or fit with the company's plans. The auditor may challenge this, but so long as you can show this was a considered, justified change in plan, you will still be in compliance with the Standard. Changing plans is not the same as abandoning or forgetting about them.

Quality Objectives

Part of your plans should be Quality Objectives. These are specifically required by the Standard to be documented, monitored, and updated.

Quality Objectives should relate to your Quality Policy. They typically relate to controlling defects, improving efficiency, meeting performance targets (including timeliness), customer satisfaction, safety, or legal requirements.

Quality Objectives can apply to your entire organisation, specific sites, or relate only to processes or activities.

For instance, you may want to reduce defects to <1%, improve the time it takes to respond to customers or complete internal processes, or make changes to prepare for legal changes.

Like all objectives, Quality Objectives should be SMART. It is critical that you monitor them regularly (depending on the goal, this could be monthly, daily or even hourly), and document your findings. This is one of the few documents you will have to show the auditor, so have it ready.

Planning changes to your Quality Management System (QMS)

Like your goals and Quality Objectives; change is not a bad thing, but it should be considered and well-thought-out. Your organisation may change structure, add a new division, or launch a new range; thus thus expanding your scope.

You will need to demonstrate that these changes have been considered, and the risks and opportunities evaluated; Top Management will need to be present on the day to discuss the decision-making process, and should show meeting minutes (not necessarily word-for-word, but enough to show actions and decisions) to support that it has been considered and is in line with company goals, risks and opportunities.

Section Seven - Support

You have established your company, and departments', objectives and how you plan to achieve them, now Top Management have to support them to DO.

This means determining and providing the resources needed.

Customer Service will need enough resources to meet their goals. How many resources? You decide, but auditors will look for evidence it is appropriate. If your organisation has a goal to have zero customer enquiries at the end of the day, but from your reports that you can see rarely meet these targets; do you have enough staff? Are they being supported, and trained sufficiently?

Is the infrastructure sufficient also; do they have enough space to work? You may have ten Warehouse staff, but if they are missing targets because they only have one forklift, their resources do not appear to be appropriate.

Is the infrastructure also safe? The auditor,

depending on their expertise, may challenge you on how you are meeting your Health and Safety legal requirements.

Expect and Encourage Competence

> Your organisation must have documented information as evidence of competence; for instance, a yearly performance review.

Support your Quality Management System by ensuring people are competent; but remember, it is up to you to determine what competence is, get people to that Standard, and measure it to make sure you are.

Awareness and Communication

The organisation should be aware of the Quality Management System, relevant to them, their contributions and the effects of not conforming.

For instance, Customer Service should be aware that they contribute by helping customers, they have a Quality Objective to respond promptly, and if they don't, this will negatively affect customers, sales and reputation of the organisation.

In preparation of the audit, remind your team of relevant Quality Objectives, and refresh them on their contributions to the Quality Management System. If they have any questions about quality, remind them that you (most likely) are the person to talk to.

Control

Controlling how you communicate your Quality Management System also needs to be considered. Most organisational staff should not be able to create and amend Quality Management documents, such as the Quality Policy, Quality Objective documents, or SOPs. So, when sharing electronic Work Instructions or Standard Operating Procedures, send them in a format that cannot be edited.

Document Control used to be a big pain, which has gotten easier with technology. There used to be a lot of mandatory documentation, and paper copies were required. Now, you can use digital copies and control who can edit them, and add a note "Uncontrolled if Printed" to the bottom - this means that staff know when something has been printed, it might not be the most up to date version.

> "Documented" doesn't mean paper, electronic documents are acceptable

Section 8 - Operations

If the previous section was about supporting your processes, this section is about controlling them.

Your processes are how you do what you do; your products and the services you provide.

Top Management develops, implements and controls your organisation's process.

This includes design, production and monitoring suppliers.

It is the broadest section and applies to all departments. Although it is the longest, it also requires the least explanation; as it is about what your organisation's processes.

Nonconformities

These must be documented.

Nonconformity is a non-fulfilment or failure to meet a requirement. A requirement is a need, expectation, or obligation. It can be stated or implied by an organization or interested parties.

Generally speaking, this would be a faulty product, a customer complaint, and failure of your suppliers or a failure to meet targets. Your documents must include the root causes; the corrective and preventative actions you have taken to stop recurrence; and an evaluation of the effectiveness of your actions.

Section Nine - Evaluation

So you have your plans, and you are putting them into action; you will need to know how you are doing.

The auditor will ask for your measures of success; customer complaints, turnaround time, defects etc and ask you to demonstrate these measures. Remember; plan what you do, do what you plan. It does not matter if your measures are taken daily, monthly or quarterly, so long as they are appropriate, and that you can demonstrate you are following through with these measures.

Internal Audits

Your organisation is also required to conduct internal audits. These should be at intervals determined by you, depending on your organisation's size and complexity.

It is a good idea to divide the audit department-by-department and follow your process through; you might start with the design of the product, through to its sale, to Customer Service accepting the order, Purchasing buy the goods, Quality testing them, and then finally Warehouse receiving and shipping them.

Or, you could follow the PDCA cycle; as we have seen, the Standard is mostly structured chronologically.

Internal Audits should be done at least annually. The frequency may increase if your internal audit results show major weaknesses in one department: for instance, if the Warehouse are found not be compliant with your organisation's processes, it would be good to consider increasing the frequency of the audit.

Who does the audit? Whoever maintains the Quality Management System; which would most likely be yourself.

To prepare the audit, go through the Standard determine how clauses apply to each

> Remember, you cannot audit your own work, so you will need to train one or more people on auditing.
>
> They will audit processes related to Quality and other departments you assist with.

department.

The internal audit schedule can be based on the external audit schedule. If you know the next audit will focus on Warehouse, make this your priority and schedule the Internal Audit beforehand. Schedule it close enough to the external audit to make sure the information you get from the Warehouse is relevant, however, leave yourself enough time to correct any problems identified in the internal audit.

Reviewing your Quality Management System

This should be done with Top Management, at least annually, and the minutes and actions must be documented and cover all clauses of the Standard (9.1.3).

The best way to ensure that this is done is to use the Standard as your agenda: make sure you minute something against them, even if there are no actions.

Section Ten - Improvement

Continuous improvement is key, and differentiates ISO 9001 from other industry-specific standards. You must work to improve your organisation's products, processes, services or customer satisfaction. The auditor will ask what your goals are, how you plan to meet them, if you are on track, and will look for evidence that these are considered and evidence-based.

Consider creating Quality Objectives, described in Section 6. These must be documented and regularly updated. Use this checklist from the Standard to ensure compliance.

- ❖ Be consistent with your Quality Policy
- ❖ Be measurable
- ❖ Take into account applicable requirements
- ❖ Be monitored (and documented)
- ❖ Be communicated
- ❖ Be updated as appropriate
- ❖ Be relevant to conformity of products/services and enhancement of customer satisfaction

You will also need to document non-conformities (Section Eight), and take steps to control these; your

Corrective Actions; and other ways to enhance your Quality Management System.

PREPARING FOR THE AUDIT

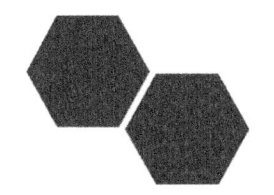

THE MANDATORY PARTS

Since the transition from ISO 9001:2008 to 2015, fewer documents are required by the Standard. This reflects how widely used the Standard is, but also how paperless offices are much more common compared to the mid-00s.

Still, some documentation is required, and if you cannot produce them on the day of the audit, you will not be in compliance, which means you are open to nonconformities.

Keep in mind, documentation can be electronic; gone are the days of a paper Quality Manual with dozens of printed SOPs. It is perfectly valid to keep Quality Management Meeting minutes in a cloud document, or training SOPs on a CRM program.

Consider using the following section as a checklist to help with your preparation and training.

You must be able to produce:

Clause	Requirement
4.1	Evidence that you have considered your organisation's context
4.2	Evidence that you have considered the needs and expectations of interested parties
4.3	The Scope of your Quality Management System (QMS)
4.4.2	Sufficient documentation to support your operations, and enough evidence to support that these are being carried out as planned.
5.2	Quality Policy
6.2	Quality Objectives - what, who, when and why, and SMART.

Clause	Requirement
7.1.5.1	Documented evidence of the monitoring and measurements you feel require
7.1.5.2	When measurement is required, you may be asked for evidence of calibration or verification
7.5.1	Information required for staff competence (SOPs, Technical Drawings)
7.5.2, 7.5.3	Evidence of document control to ensure that any required documents in circulation are the correct version and can only be updated and amended by appropriate people, and how it is stored, distributed, controlled, retained and destroyed.
8.1, 7.5.1	Documents required for your Operations and to show conformity of your products
8.4.1	Evidence of supplier control, for the evaluation, selection, monitoring of performance, and re-evaluation of external providers, based on their ability to provide processes or products and services in accordance with requirements - this includes any Corrective Actions required based on this performance monitoring
8.5.1	Documents required for product or service control such as Technical Drawings or Training SOPs.
8.5.2	Evidence of traceability and the testing of traceability (certain industries require traceability of batch numbers or even raw materials, you must be able to provide evidence of this traceability, and evidence that traceability has been tested appropriately.)

Clause	Requirement
8.5.3	Documents of any damage that has occurred to customer or supplier property
8.5.6	Documented evidence of the control of change if your products change, you must provide evidence that you have informed the supplier, and customer etc.
8.6	Evidence of conformity and traceability when releasing goods; you determine if the goods are acceptable to be released, and who released them.
8.7.2	Evidence of control of nonconformities including description and corrective actions taken, and how effective they were. Auditors will **always** ask about nonconformities so make sure they are well documented, up-to-date, and close as many as possible.
9.1, 9.2	Internal audits and any results of reviews that you feel are appropriate and required (9.1, 9.2) Auditors will always look at Internal Audits, so make sure they are prepared and any resulting actions are closed,
9.3	Management review, including actions and minutes; they must cover all the items listed in clause 9.3.2

You must also be prepared to *talk* about:

- ❖ Your organisation, history, products and culture.
- ❖ Your Quality Management System, what it is, who runs it, how do you manage it (e.g. cloud, paper, lots of SOPs, or only a few)
- ❖ How Top Leadership support the Quality Management System and Customer Focus
- ❖ How people in the organisation know what they are doing (job specs, training, etc.)
- ❖ How the company identifies and tackles risks and opportunities, and changes
- ❖ The organisation's people, training and resources and the knowledge required
- ❖ How the organisation communicates its Quality Management System; how do staff know about the Quality Policy, what a nonconformity is, etc., and who is responsible for the communications.

> The audit may be the first time your auditor has ever heard of your company, they will want to get to know you. Find someone who can speak authoritatively and knowledgeably about the company.

- ❖ Your processes of operations, product requirements, how you determine customer requirements and how you communicate with them.
- ❖ Supplier selection, how you communicate with them and your expectations of them

PREPARING YOUR TEAM

Even if you are the only one responsible for the audit, you can't do this alone; you will need support from Top Management and department heads leading up to the audit, and on the day.

It is unlikely you will be audited on every process each audit. Beforehand, the auditing body will send you a schedule of which processes and/or departments they will focus on.

An example:

11:00	Order Processing
12:00	Lunch
12:30	Purchasing
13:30	Goods In/Goods Out

From the schedule, you can see that Customer Service (who process orders) and the Warehouse (who handle goods in/goods out) will be needed for the audit, along with the Purchasing department. So in your preparations, you will need to include the heads of these departments. The audit will also speak with them on the day.

As part of your preparations, train your auditees on what will happen on the day, and some basic audit skills, which we will cover in the next section.

In addition to the department heads, the auditor may also want to speak with amore junior employee who performs the processes every day; to verify that what the managers are saying is correct. Before the audit, have someone in mind that is experienced and positive to pick, should the auditor ask.

Choosing your Team

You should include Top Management, department heads, and relevant staff who are friendly, chatty, experienced, and especially, **positive**. They can make the difference!

> One auditor was particularly grumpy in the morning. However, the Customer Service Team Leaders at the time were very amiable, in addition to being smart and effective at their roles.
>
> After a tense morning, the auditor was more pleasant in the afternoon after speaking with the Team Leaders.

The Day Of

Auditors are different, and so are auditing bodies, however, audits should follow the same basic structure.

Opening Meeting

Auditors will introduce themselves and explain

the plan for the day.

Have the relevant department heads ready to introduce themselves also, along with at least one representative of Top Management present. Don't throw anyone in at the deep-end though; these should all be people you have prepared for today and imparted some audit skills.

Previous Findings

The auditor will discuss any minor nonconformities from the previous audit to see that they have been addressed, and preferably, closed. It is very bad news not to have done so, so make sure you have prepared and documented your Corrections (solving the problem) Root Cause Analysis, Corrective Actions and evidence that the actions you have taken have been successful. **These must be documented.**

Scope and Exclusions

This is what is included in the purview of the audit, and what is not. Exclusions should be determined and documented beforehand. If you do not design and develop products in your organisation, you can exclude clauses 8.3 from your scope. It may be that you are part of a bigger corporation, and your site only performs certain functions: in which case you would exclude any processes (and clauses) that are not done at your site, even if they are done elsewhere in the organisation.

Remember, you set the scope; you can include as many processes and products as you like. If you have added multiple, distinct product lines, you can choose which ones to include and which ones not to; so long as you consider this before the audit and document it. Otherwise, the auditor will look for compliance to clauses, and if you cannot demonstrate compliance, you could receive an otherwise avoidable non-conformity.

When discussing this Scope, use this opportunity to introduce the auditor to your organisation, culture, structure, product line and services.

Having someone knowledgeable and loquacious present to talk to the auditor can help a great deal. It will help the auditor understand the organisation, and in your favour; the more time the auditor spends listening, the less time they can spend asking questions.

They will also ask to see your Quality Policy, which must be documented, so be familiar with this and have it ready.

Objectives and Goals

The auditor will ask about the objectives of the company; this could include the financial goals, the markets you are targeting, new product lines. Top Management should host this section; as they will be able to speak more authoritatively and about aspects of the business you may not be familiar with.

Anything discussed in an audit is under non-disclosure agreement, so if management has any OGSM presentations (objectives, goals, strategies and measures) they may help explain your strategy, and also indicating that your organisation sets goals and follows through with them.

Remember, it is acceptable to set a target for improvement and not meet it, so long as you have taken appropriate steps towards it, and assessed why it has not been met. It is not acceptable to set an improvement target and then abandon it, without justification.

This includes Quality Objectives.

Department-by-Department, Process-by-Process

We then move on to the meat of the audit; processes and departments.

It is very unlikely you will need everyone for each section of the audit; usually one, two or three key people; along with yourself. If you have too many people, they will either get bored, or it will increase the chance someone may say something they are not supposed to, or perhaps not entirely knowledgeable about.

You will have thought beforehand about who should be involved in each part of the audit, so as it progresses, you will thank your current auditees for their time, then excuse yourself to go and retrieve your next auditees.

Top Management will most likely be required for the broader goals and objectives of the company. As you move on, you should call upon the relevant department heads. The auditor may want to speak with more junior employees as they go; again, think beforehand about who best to call on should this happen, and train them on what to expect.

Lunch

It is unlikely auditors will want to extend their day by taking a long lunch off-site, but you will want to arrange lunch for today. Remember to ask ahead of time if they have any dietary requirements.

Invite your auditees to lunch too: to thank them for their participation, and also allow the auditor opportunity to bond with you and your team more informally. Having a pleasant relationship with them can never hurt.

Report Preparation and/or Closing Meeting

Following the audit part of the audit, the auditor will conduct the closing meeting. They will summarise their findings, good and bad, and give examples of good practice and any nonconformities or observations that they identified. There should be no surprises in the closing meeting; the auditor will alert you to their findings as they go. Equally, this is not the time for you to bring anything new to the audit.

The auditor will likely schedule your next audit, including their schedule, and be on their way. Then you can relax, and congratulate yourself on a successful audit. Your final report should arrive within a few days.

How to Prepare, Perform, and Pass an ISO 9001 2015 audit

TIPS FOR THE DAY AND AUDIT SKILLS

This final section will give you tips for the day as the host, and some audit skills that you can share with your team during their preparation and training.

First Impressions

Auditors see all sorts of companies, with varying levels of interest in ISO 9001:2015. If you can make a good first impression and indicate that you are taking the audit seriously, it will give them confidence that you are taking the Standard seriously also.

Having Top Management and relevant department heads present for the opening meeting, clearly prepared and enthusiastic, will go a long way.

If the auditor gets the sense in the morning that you are taking things seriously and are generally compliant, they may have in the back of their mind leaving a little early so they can beat the traffic.

Don't waste time… but there is no need to rush

Audits are a marathon, not a sprint, and the auditor is there for a set amount of time. You don't want to waste their time, but there is no harm in burning a few minutes here and there.

For instance, when you go to retrieve your next auditee, leave to go and get them from their desk rather than summon them by phone. This will also give you both a few minutes to regain your composure. Be generous with offering tea and coffee, and invite your auditees to lunch; especially the chatty ones. Encourage your auditees to take their time during their introductions in the Opening Meeting, and Top Management should speak loquaciously when describing and introducing the organisation.

There is an art to knowing that when you are on the right track with an auditor and you can keep talking without saying anything "incriminating", and when to give concise answers only. This will come to you and your auditees with time and experience.

What follows is the general rule-of-thumb for how to answer, particularly for more junior employees without audit-experience:

Introduction	Open Questions	Closed Questions
Take your time at the beginning to introduce yourself and your role; be broad.	"How do you train new starters?" Give broad, high-level answers, avoiding specifics.	"Do you monitor KPIs?" Be short, concise and relevant,

Answer the question, but don't offer information

This is particularly true for more junior employees, who may feel nervous talking to an auditor and feel the need to fill any gaps. Use the example to demonstrate what this means:

"Do you have a watch?"

~~"Yes, it is 11:15"~~
"Yes, I do"

If the auditor asks you a closed question, such as *"do you audit traceability of your raw materials"*, the answer is not:

"yes, twice per year, last was in March or May time, the next one is due in the summer, last time we found this... here's the report"

... it is simply:

"yes, we do".

If the auditor wants to know how often and when, and they probably do, they will ask. It is their job is to ask questions though, so let them. There may be silences in the conversation; either the auditor may deliberately pause to see if you offer more information, or they may be taking notes, but don't be compelled to continue talking to just fill the gap. Instead, smile.

Not only does this reduce the risk of an auditee perhaps saying something they are unsure about, but also avoids the auditor misunderstanding or half-hearing something. Also, it helps run down the clock.

Tell, don't show (until you are asked)

Similar to the previous point, avoid the temptation to reach for your laptop or folder of documents whenever the auditor asks a question. They may want to see your traceability audit from last May, but wait for them to ask. Auditor's Luck means that the one record you pull up will have something wrong with it; so it is best to wait for the auditor to ask to see a report, rather than offer it.

If you spot an error, don't point it out!

Again, this is particularly for junior-employees who may prefer to get ahead of an error, rather than wait for an auditor to call it out for them. Although it seems obvious, auditees should avoid this temptation.

Firstly, you are the expert in your organisation;

an obvious error to you may not be obvious to the auditor.

Secondly, if they are looking at who conducted an internal audit, for instance, they may not see that the date on the report is incorrect. Why bring it to their attention?

Finally, this principle applies to negative comments in general. If the auditor is looking at an account with Customer Service, the representative should avoid the temptation to say that "we always have problems with this customer"; this just opens the doors to more questions that could have been avoided. Similarly, if Quality is looking at faulty goods reports, don't announce "this product always breaks", because then the auditor will ask why you have not given it more attention. If that is the case, you should have dealt with it in your audit preparations.

Keep in mind though, the auditor is a human too, and they understand humans make errors. No one ever failed an audit because of a single error, so tell your auditees not to fret.

Accept their suggestions, but remain non-committal

Auditors don't work for your organisation, so they can comment, but not command.

Often, auditors are experts in their field and could have valuable insights. Part of your role throughout the day is to glean any potential improvements and advice you can from the auditor; they have seen the working of more organisations than anyone could hope to work for, so there is often merit in what they say.

Take their feedback on board, but keep in mind the phrase "It's something we can look in to". Should you commit to a change, the auditor may write this in their report, meaning you are bound to at least investigate it before the next audit.

"I would ask my manager" is a perfectly acceptable answer

More junior employees may feel foolish or anxious being asked a question they do not know about, you should teach them that "I would ask my manager" is a perfectly acceptable answer. The auditor would expect staff to have some knowledge, but they would prefer to know that staff would ask for assistance, rather than just wing it.

The same principle applies to more senior employees also; they would not necessarily ask their manager, but instead would rely on other departments for knowledge. So, "I would ask the Purchasing team" or Quality, or the Legal department, are viable, and likely correct, answers.

Stay In Your Lane

When discussing departments other than their own, auditees should try their best to only answer from their own perspective, rather than speculate or narrate what other

departments

do.

For instance, if questioned what they would do with a report of a nonconforming product, each department would have a different, correct answer:

Customer Service would arrange a return and escalate to the Quality department. The Warehouse would receive the return and place it into quarantine. Purchasing may ask the supplier for credit or replacement, and Quality would investigate the root cause and corrective actions.

Answer from your own perspective

For instance, if questioned what they would do with a faulty product, each department would have a different, correct answer.

Customer Service would arrange a return and escalate to the Quality department. The Warehouse would receive the return and place it into quarantine. Purchasing may ask the supplier for credit or replacement, and Quality would investigate the root cause and corrective actions.

Auditees should answer from their own perspective, and avoid speculating on what other departments do. It opens the possibility of giving skewed, overly-simplistic, incorrect or out-dated information, and simply isn't necessary. If the auditor really wants to know, they will ask that department.

The 4 Cs: consistency, compliance, continual improvement and customer-focus

These are the key things the auditor is looking for; if your auditees get this right, if nothing else, you are on a good track.

Consistency; they want to know that the person processing an order is doing it the same way as the person sitting next to them, and how is this achieved. This could be done by training, SOPs, special-instructions, or keeping information on a shared database; among other methods.

Compliance; you do what you say you do. Your organisation is likely beholden to regulatory and legal standards, but most importantly, do what you say you do. You set your processes, KPIs, targets and objectives, you should be following them.

Continual improvement; you must demonstrate how you are making things better; for your customers, your product, your staff, the environment. Set your own goals, plan them, and follow through with them.

Customer focus; your organisation should show how you prioritise customers, and incentivise staff to do the same. Auditees should understand the consequence of no-conforming on their customers.

Finally, Accentuate the Positives

If you only have time to prepare your auditees with one lesson (and I hope that is not the case) this would be it.

It requires little explanation, and hopefully goes without saying, but do everything in you can to ensure your auditees avoid focusing on negatives. Some auditees may see an audit as a chance for them to finally be heard, and be tempted to tell someone who is listening, everything they think is wrong, but there simply could not be a worse time or place.

If an auditee identifies a problem during an auditee, the best thing to do is keep it to themselves and then bring it to your attention afterwards. Do not let them be tempted to complain about customers, products, colleagues or anything else that has been bothering them.

Negative Phrases to Avoid

"We always have problems with this product"
"This never works"
"This customer is always difficult"
"I kept saying this was a problem but no one listened"
"I raised this issue months ago and nothing happened"

Remind auditees that although no organisation is perfect, generally speaking, goods go out on time, customers reorder, you make money (hopefully) and you meet targets.

Some negative things may come up in an audit, but again, accentuate the positives and diminish the negatives:

Accentuate the Positives

"That's no problem, we can correct that straight away"
"We have had one or two complaints, but we have shipped thousands without issue, so it is not a wider trend"
"We did miss target last month, but we have done *XYZ* and we are still on track for the year"
"Something did go wrong with this order, but here's why it was an exceptional case"

Things may not be perfect, but they can be positive.

CLOSING THOUGHTS

This final lesson is for you, as the individual responsible for the audit.

I will not lie, audits are daunting things. Never in my life can I say that I have looked forward to an audit. The best you can say is that you are ready to get it out the way.

Like most things, they get easier the more you practice, but one thing always remains true, whether it is your first audit or your fifteenth:

> You don't need to panic, but you do need to prepare

Picking up this book is a great start, because if you are thinking about your upcoming ISO 9001 audit, you are already a step ahead.

The day of the audit is important, there is no doubt about that, but so is the day, the week, the month and the year before the audit, because this is your preparation time.

So, *prepare*.

Read the Standard, exclude what clauses you can, think about your organisation's objectives, pull together your Quality Management Meetings, close as many outstanding nonconformities as you can, have your Internal Audits ready, print off your Quality Policy, prepare your auditees, book lunch for the day and… do what you can. Because if you do that, there is no reason the audit will not go as smoothly as possible.

Prepare what you can, and perform on the day. I won't tell you to enjoy it, because that's pushing it too far! The best I can offer is to remind you, you don't need to panic; because by reading this, you are already getting prepared.

Best of luck.

APPENDICES

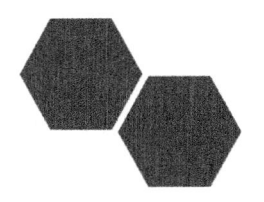

ORGANISATIONAL RISK REGISTER

A Risk Register is a Risk Management tool to identify and risks, and include additional information about the nature of the risk; its probability of occurrence, impact and detectability; mitigating factors; and planned responses.

SUPPLY &
DEMAND
CHANGES
COMPETITION
STRATEGIC
ADVANCEMENT
STRATEGY
NEW
TECHNOLOGY
MERGERS
PARTNERSHIPS
ACQUISITIONS

Strategic Risks result directly from operating within a specific industry at a specific time. Shifts in consumer preference, technology, and competition present risk. Loss may arise from the pursuit of unsuccessful business plans, poor business decisions, poor execution of decisions, inadequate resource allocation, or failure to respond well to changes in the business environment.

Operational Risks are internal failures, resulting from inadequate or failed procedures, systems, policies; or any event that disrupts business processes.

Compliance and Legal Risks are those subject to legislative or bureaucratic rule and regulations, or those associated with best practices. These can include environmental, health and safety, and product regulations; contractual agreements; employee protections; and social and quality responsibilities.

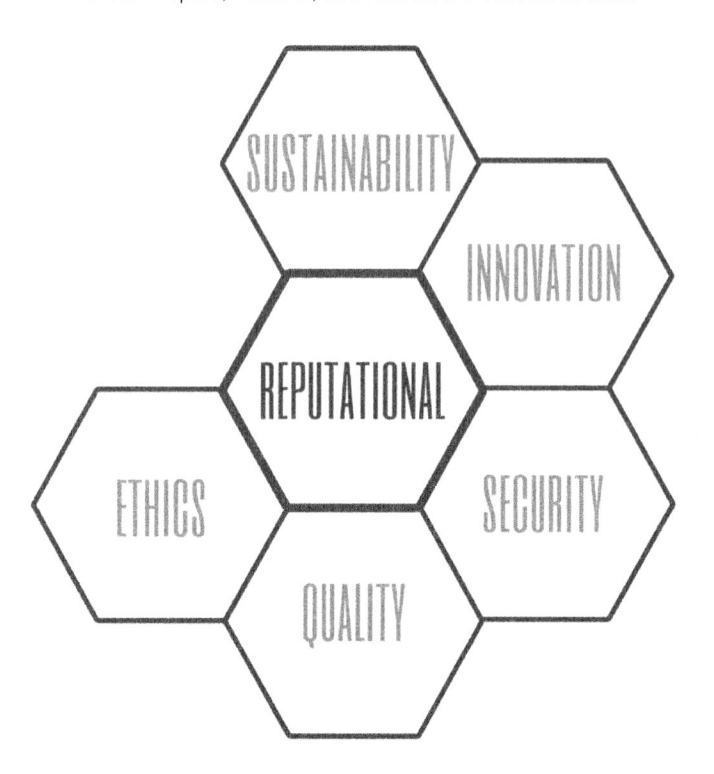

Reputational Risk is a risk of loss resulting from damages to a firm's reputation; in lost revenue, destruction of shareholder value, loss of customers or partnerships. Adverse events typically associated with reputation risk include ethics, safety, security, sustainability, quality, and innovation.

FINANCIAL: CUSTOMER CREDIT, HIGH INVENTORY, EXCHANGE RATES, SUPPLIER CREDIT

Financial Risks relate how the business handles money; for instance, how much credit is extended to customers, how much credit suppliers extend to the business, the cost of inventory and liquidity risk, and the effect of foreign exchange rates.

Other Risks are more difficult to categorize. They can include risks from external factors such as politics, the economy, the environment etc.

Documented Risk Register

Use the categories to determine and assess your risks, your existing controls and mitigating factors, planned responses, and any extra actions your organisation needs to take.

Use a Qualitative Risk Assessment Matrix to assess the probability and impact of your risks, before and after your mitigating factors. Using this you can prioritise your risks. This should be documented for the audit and reviewed at least annually.

INTERESTED PARTIES

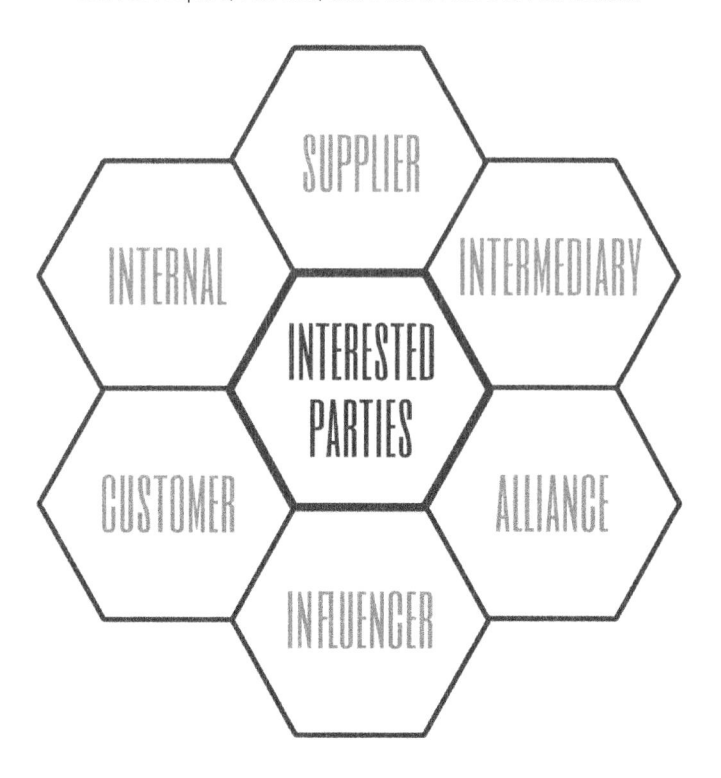

Use the Six Markets Model as guidance to identify your Interested Parties. Use the Power/Interest Matrix to prioritise your Interested Parties; the higher they are rated, the more effort required to meet their needs are expectations.

Interested Parties

CUSTOMER buyers, end users

SUPPLIER vendors, contractors utilities, landlords

INTERMEDIARY hauliers, couriers recruitment

ALLIANCE partners

INFLUENCER pressure groups reviewers, media

INTERNAL management, staff

OTHER regulators, legislators, neighbours, community

Power can be interpreted as their significance or risk. Interest can be interpreted as the strength of their relevance.

Use different research methods as necessary to confirm knowledge of each group. Define how we can meet these needs; how we will determine if these actions are effective; if our actions are successful; and if further actions are needed.

This should be documented for the audit and reviewed at least annually.

ABOUT THE AUTHOR

Rhys Mitchell has worked as part of the Quality team in ISO 9001:2008 and ISO 9001:2015 companies for over 10 years

This is what started as a loose collection of thoughts on how to perform during audits, which evolved into general advice to give to colleague; into brief notes, into training presentations; and finally into this, book.

Printed in Great Britain
by Amazon